HIDE AND SEEK
FIRST WORDS

A Dorling Kindersley Book

Notes for parents

Hide-and-seek First Words is a great picture book for you and your child to share. Filled with all sorts of wonderful objects to find and talk about, this book will help your child build vocabulary, learn colours, practise counting, and develop observation skills.

To get the most out of this book

- Talk about all the things you can see on each page. Point to the objects, say their names, then hunt for each one together. As children become familiar with the book, they will be able to name and find the objects themselves.

- Encourage your child to describe the different things. What colour or shape are they? What are they made of? Which one is your child's favourite? Do you have something similar at home?

- Read the rhymes and let your child say them with you. Then help your child find the objects in the rhymes.

- Once your child knows letter sounds, you can play traditional "I spy". Ask your child to spot an object on the page that begins with a certain letter.

DK

LONDON, NEW YORK,
MELBOURNE, MUNICH, AND DELHI

Written by Dawn Sirett
Designed by Rachael Parfitt and Victoria Palastanga
Special Photography by Dave King
Illustrations by Rachael Parfitt and Victoria Palastanga
Production Controller Louise Kelly
Production Editor Andy Hilliard

First published in Great Britain in 2010
by Dorling Kindersley Limited,
80 Strand, London WC2R 0RL

Copyright © 2010 Dorling Kindersley Limited

A Penguin Company
10 9 8 7 6 5 4 3
012–175769–Jun/10

A CIP catalogue record for this book is available
from the British Library.

ISBN: 978-1-40535-173-7

Printed and bound in China
by Leo Paper Products

Discover more at
www.dk.com

a dump truck

a pair of sparkly shoes

a spinning top

a rubber ring

a motorbike

a watering can

Contents

a polo shirt

a clock

a woolly hat

a xylophone

Boo!

This is Buzzy Bee. He's on every page of this book! See if you can spot him again and again.

Toy shelf

Let's find...

 a duck

 a teddy

 a ball

 a train

 a doll

 a tower of stacking cups

 a camera

 a spinning top

 a jar of marbles

 a penguin

 an elephant

 a caterpillar

 a snail

 a drum

 a crocodile

 a cat

 a rocket

 3 wooden people

 2 fire engines

 a fire fighter

 a robot

 a dinosaur

 a hobby horse

I spy a racing car.
If you see it, you're a star!

Clothes
Let's find...

some pyjamas

a vest

a pair of pants

a dressing gown

a pair of slippers

2 jumpers

a pair of dungarees

a pair of trainers

a watch

a dress

a skirt

a jacket

a scarf

a pair of trousers

a pair of socks

a pair of sparkly shoes

a hairbrush

a comb

2 white buttons

a belt

a raincoat

an umbrella

6

Choose your
favourite thing to wear,
then find a little
teddy bear.

Animals

Let's find...

an elephant

a spider

a giraffe

a dinosaur

a horse

a mouse

a kangaroo and joey

a dog

a lion

a hippo

2 snakes

3 ducks

a zebra

a pig

a crocodile

a cow

a frog

a rabbit

8

Which creature
has been caught
for lunch?
Can he escape
before he's
munched?

9

In the garden

Let's find...

a butterfly

a trowel

3 snails

4 bulbs

a spider

a stripy plant pot

a yellow watering can

a ball of string

a dragonfly

3 ladybirds

a frog

a fork

a pair of gloves

2 sunflowers

a bird

a bird house

a rake

a pair of wellies

10

Can you see a tiny man with his own small watering can?

Colours

Let's find...

a green paintbrush

a red lipstick

a man in blue

a yellow bus

an orange flower

a green leaf

a purple comb

a green bug

a red mouse

a purple butterfly

12

a yellow chick

 an orange bracelet

 1 green circle

 3 orange triangles

 2 blue rectangles

 a blue dinosaur

 a red strawberry

 3 yellow squares

 7 purple stars

 1 red heart

If you can find a tiny bed, you'll spot a teeny sleepyhead!

13

Play school

Let's find...

a painting

a pair of scissors

a pencil case

a frog calculator

a skipping rope

3 crayons

a ruler

a pencil sharpener

a stapler

a football rubber

3 tubes of glitter

a blackboard

a pair of glasses

a pen

a paint palette

3 paintbrushes

a piece of chalk

a magnet

3 red stars

a glue pen

a magnifying glass

a clock

4 bottles of paint

2 toy children

a notebook

a globe

I spy a little cat somewhere.
It was made at school
with great care.

Spots and stripes

Let's find...

a present

a doggy rattle

5 red-and-white toadstools

a caterpillar

a leopard

a domino

a fish

a red-and-whit bow

a rainbow
purse

a notebook

4 pencils

a pair
of mittens

a rainbow

a tiger

a plate

a cup
and saucer

a woolly hat

a dice

a teddy

Meow! Meow! Who said that? Where's the stripy knitted cat?

At the **beach**

Let's find...

a sandcastle

2 sailing boats

a kite

a pair of sandals

a cap

a pair of binoculars

a swimming costume

a bucket

a dolphin

a flag

a pair of swimming trunks

a spade

4 pebbles

a pair of flippers

a pair of sunglasses

an ice-cream

a rubber ring

a snorkel

a mask

a windmill

Somewhere
at the beach I spy
a scaly turtle creeping by.

19

In the kitchen

Let's find...

a mug

a colander

a grater

a kettle

a vase of flowers

3 spoons

a clock

a box of tissues

a bowl of fruit

a framed photo

a blue jug

a spatula

a tea towel

a pair of tongs

3 bowls

a vegetable peeler

a casserole dish

a washing-up brush

3 hooks

a blue serving spoon

a sieve

2 keys

a tray

a saucepan

I spy two big eyes and a mouth so wide you can fit a kitchen sponge inside!

Things that go

Let's find...

a motorbike

2 blue-and-red planes

a hot-air balloon

a sailing boat

2 orange-and-green racing cars

3 red cars

a jeep

a scooter

a tractor with loader

a helicopter

a truck

a rubbish truck

a bus

a fire engine

Look at all
the things to drive,
then find the number 55.

Play cooking

Let's find...

a jar
of jam

a blue
mixing bowl

3 biscuits

a rolling pin

a heart
pastry cutter

4 pink iced cakes

4 pasta shapes

a jelly
mould

a spoon

a knife

an oven
glove

a fork

4 empty cake cases

a wooden
spoon

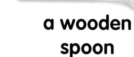
some raisins

a whisk

a weighing
scale

a cake stand

24

Spot three candles
on three cakes,
and two hearts
cut out to bake.

Busy builders

Let's find...

7 stripy cones

a tipper truck

a wheel loader

a backhoe loader

2 drills

a bulldozer

One busy builder has a call from home. Can you see the mobile phone?

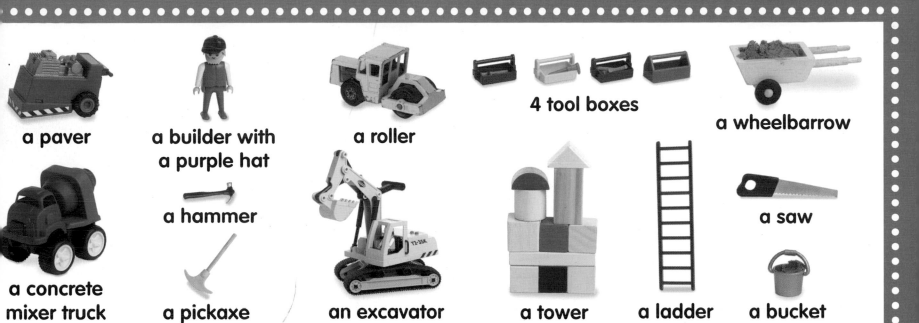

a paver

a builder with a purple hat

a roller

4 tool boxes

a wheelbarrow

a concrete mixer truck

a hammer

a pickaxe

an excavator

a tower

a ladder

a saw

a bucket

Black and white

Let's find...

a magician's wand

a bow tie

a rabbit

a pair of
glasses

2 wheels

a polar bear

a pair of shoes

a piano

2 ghosts

a panda

Find a mouse
playing
a tune,
and a couple
marrying soon!

a skeleton

a blackbird

an egg

3 bats

a plastic hat

a cauldron

8 dominoes

a monkey

3 footballs

3 black cats

a Dalmatian

29

Bathtime

Let's find...

a fishing net

a butterfly soap

a bottle of shampoo

a yellow towel

a crab

a soap dish

a mermaid

a bottle of bubble bath

a nailbrush

a starfish

a seal

a seahorse

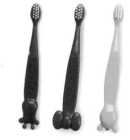
3 toothbrushes

a big yellow duck

a blue-and-yellow diver

2 green boats

Look here, there...

...and everywhere
for six bubbles
in the air.

Doll's house

Let's find...

a bath

2 pink chairs

a bike

a lamp

a toaster

a bunk bed

a rabbit hutch

a green chest of drawers

a sofa

a shower

a table

Dad, Mum, 2 children, and the baby

a kitchen sink

a highchair

a saucepan

a train

a television

a computer

a cooker

a pram

a rocking horse

a bed

a toilet

2 big windows

a cot

32

I spy with my little eye
a dog and a rabbit, and a cat up high.

33

On the farm

Let's find...

4 ducklings

2 cows

2 sheep

a tractor

a donkey

2 farmers

4 hens

a cockerel

4 horses

2 milk churns

a basket of vegetables

a dog

a kennel

a tyre

a turkey

a kid

a goat

a pitchfork

a pig

2 piglets

a pigsty

a green ladder

Somewhere hiding
for you to seek,
are three farm mice.
Squeak, squeak, squeak!

35

Musical things
Let's find...

a recorder

a trumpet

2 cymbals

a xylophone

2 shakers

a triangle

8 gold bells

a drum

2 harmonicas

a bongo drum

an accordion

a tambourine

3 kazoos

an electric guitar

a keyboard

Spy a
frog that goes
click click. You
can do it – you're
so quick!

37

Story time

Let's find...

the Queen

the King

a dragon

a witch's cat

a glass slipper

2 ballerinas

a horse and carriage

a tower

38

a witch

2 princesses

a fairy godmother

the moon

2 fairies

3 fish

a lion

a prince

a mermaid

a superhero

a wizard

Spot two magic wands, then here's what you do...

...make a special wish that you'd like to come true!

Treasure hunt

Let's find...

a treasure chest

a key

a parrot

a crown

a pirate ship

a gold buckle

a green heart jewel

6 wooden pirates

a charm bracelet

a monkey

10 gold coins

a brooch

a fob watch

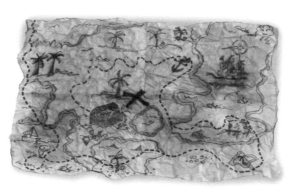
a treasure map

a sword

a book

a compass

a quill pen

a starfish

a telescope

a ruby ring

a scroll

a pirate's hat

More sparkly jewels are buried in the ground.
I spy the "X" where they can be found!

Numbers

Let's find the number...

 **zero**
 one
 two
 **three**
 **four**
 **five**

six
seven
eight
nine
ten
eleven

 **twelve**
 thirteen
 fourteen
fifteen
 **sixteen**
 seventeen

 **eighteen**
 **nineteen**
twenty
 **fifty**
 **one hundred**

Now let's count...

2 rainbows

2 green stars

3 yellow planets

5 candles

How old are you? Please tell me.
And where's that number? Can you see?

Christmas

Let's find...

a penguin

a Christmas tree

a tiny Santa

an owl

a red spotty bauble

a dancing Santa

2 candy canes

a teddy

a sledge and rider

a spotty star

an angel

2 snowmen

3 blue sweets

2 pinecones

a reindeer

a stocking

5 green baubles

44

Find a letter. Who's it to?
What would you write
if it was from you?

45

More to find!

You'll find all these things if you go back and look at the big, busy pictures in this hide-and-seek book!

a lemon

a mirror

a red
spotty kettle

a police car

a saxophone

3 skateboards

a yellow spatula

a cake slice

an orange
cat clock

a bookshelf

a yellow
concrete mixer

a car transporter

2 cowboys

2 oranges

a slice of
orange

a pair
of tights

a green
tractor

a tomato

a bag of flour

a pirate skull
eyepatch

Bye-bye!

4 blue spotty clouds

a coat stand

a deckchair

a broom

a red cotton reel

a silver whistle

3 suns

a bird and birdcage

an apple tree

7 more trees

a torch

a little chef

a yellow sponge

a packet of seeds

an armchair

2 red sweets

a rose ring

an abacus

a dog bowl

a bale of wheat

Index of words we've found!